BRITANNICA BEGINNER BIOS

NELSON MANDELA

NOBEL PEACE PRIZE–WINNING CHAMPION
FOR HOPE AND HARMONY

TRACEY BAPTISTE

Britannica
Educational Publishing

IN ASSOCIATION WITH

ROSEN
EDUCATIONAL SERVICES

Published in 2016 by Britannica Educational Publishing (a trademark of Encyclopædia Britannica, Inc.) in association with The Rosen Publishing Group, Inc.
29 East 21st Street, New York, NY 10010

Distributed exclusively by Rosen Publishing.
To see additional Britannica Educational Publishing titles, go to rosenpublishing.com.

First Edition

Britannica Educational Publishing
J.E. Luebering: Director, Core Reference Group
Mary Rose McCudden: Editor, Britannica Student Encyclopedia

Rosen Publishing
Hope Lourie Killcoyne: Executive Editor
Meredith Day: Editor
Nelson Sá: Art Director
Michael Moy: Designer
Cindy Reiman: Photography Manager
Karen Huang: Photo Researcher

Library of Congress Cataloging-in-Publication Data

Baptiste, Tracey.
Nelson Mandela: Nobel Peace Prize–winning champion for hope and harmony/Tracey Baptiste.
       pages cm.—(Britannica beginner bios)
Includes bibliographical references and index.
ISBN 978-1-62275-941-5 (library bound)—ISBN 978-1-62275-942-2 (pbk.)—ISBN 978-1-62275-944-6 (6-pack)
1. Mandela, Nelson, 1918–2013—Juvenile literature. 2. Presidents—South Africa—Biography—Juvenile literature. 3. Political prisoners—South Africa—Biography—Juvenile literature. 4. Apartheid—Juvenile literature. I. Title.
DT1974.B36 2016
968.06'5092—dc23
[B]
                                                                                              2014039765

Manufactured in the United States of America

CONTENTS

Chapter 1
WHO WAS NELSON MANDELA?   4

Chapter 2
BIRTH OF A TROUBLEMAKER   8

Chapter 3
POLITICAL LIFE   12

Chapter 4
PRISONER NUMBER 46664   18

Chapter 5
PRESIDENT MANDELA   23

Timeline   29
Glossary   30
For More Information   31
Index   32

CHAPTER ONE

WHO WAS NELSON MANDELA?

Nelson Mandela was the first black president of South Africa. He was a great leader. Many people admired him for his forgiveness and courage.

Nelson Mandela is pictured here in 1990 shortly after being released from prison.

Setting an Example

For many years, black people in South Africa were not treated fairly. Most of the people in the country were black, but white people controlled the government. The government made laws that said where blacks could live and work. Blacks were not allowed to own land or to travel freely. The laws were part of a system called apartheid. The government used apartheid to keep people of different races separated.

This whites-only sign was displayed at a beach in South Africa.

Quick Fact

The word *apartheid* means "apartness" in Afrikaans. Afrikaans is a language spoken in South Africa. It developed from the language of Dutch people who came there in the 1600s.

Mandela and others protested to end apartheid laws. Mandela was sent to jail for life. But in 1990, after 27 years, he was freed.

South Africa was deeply divided. After Mandela became president, he tried to set an example. He worked for peace and unity.

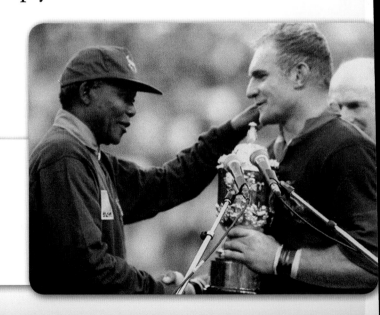

Mandela encouraged unity by supporting the Springboks, the national rugby team, during the 1995 Rugby World Cup. At the time, the team was white only.

Vocabulary

HUMAN RIGHTS are the rights that belong to everyone, such as the right to freedom, the right to live, and the right to believe what one chooses.

Life After Politics

Mandela served only one five-year term as president. After that he worked with groups that promoted peace and **HUMAN RIGHTS**. He wanted to solve many problems, such as disease and world poverty.

After he died, people felt a great loss.

CHAPTER TWO

BIRTH OF A TROUBLEMAKER

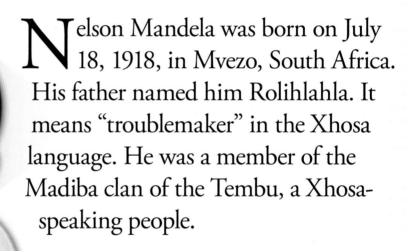

Nelson Mandela was born on July 18, 1918, in Mvezo, South Africa. His father named him Rolihlahla. It means "troublemaker" in the Xhosa language. He was a member of the Madiba clan of the Tembu, a Xhosa-speaking people.

A Royal Family

Nelson Mandela's father was a chief of the Tembu people. He

Mandela is pictured here in 1950 wearing traditional Tembu clothing.

Quick Fact

South Africa has eleven official languages. Nine of them are Bantu languages that have been spoken since before European settlers came to South Africa. One of the Bantu languages is Xhosa.

settled arguments and advised other chiefs. One day, Mandela's father argued with a white law official about some cattle. The man took away the chief's job. Even as a chief, a black man did not have much power. Mandela's family had to leave their home.

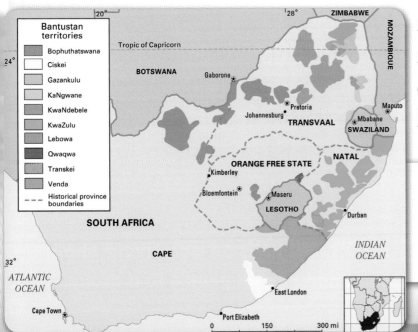

Bantustan territories

Bophuthatswana
Ciskei
Gazankulu
KaNgwane
KwaNdebele
KwaZulu
Lebowa
Qwaqwa
Transkei
Venda
Historical province boundaries

During the apartheid era, blacks in South Africa were forced to live in areas called Bantustan territories.

They went to live in a country village called Qunu.

Mandela loved the country. He played stick fighting. He herded the family's sheep and goats. At age seven, he was sent to school. His teacher gave him a new name: Nelson.

When Mandela was still a child, his father died. He was sent to the home of an even greater chief, Jongintaba. The chief's house was called the Great Place. At tribal meetings, the chief listened to arguments. The chief allowed everyone to participate and to come to a **CONSENSUS** together. Mandela learned this was a good way to lead.

Mandela wears a traditional Xhosa hat in his village of Qunu in 2000.

Vocabulary
A **CONSENSUS** is an agreement about something by all people in a group.

At age sixteen, Mandela went through a traditional **COMING-OF-AGE CEREMONY**. Men told stories at the ceremony. Mandela learned that the Xhosa people were once powerful. Then

Mandela's grandson Bambatha Mandela (covered in a blanket) takes part in the Xhosa coming-of-age ceremony.

Europeans took over the country. After that the Xhosa were poor and powerless. The speeches changed him.

Vocabulary

A COMING-OF-AGE CEREMONY marks the introduction of young people into the world of adults.

CHAPTER THREE

POLITICAL LIFE

Mandela began to think more about the way blacks were treated in South Africa. He worked hard at his schoolwork and did well as a result. He went to the only university that blacks were allowed to attend. In his second year at the school, he was forced to leave because he joined in a protest.

Life in Johannesburg

He returned to his home. Chief Jongintaba arranged a marriage for him. Mandela did not want to marry. He ran away to Johannesburg. There, he found work as a guard in the mines.

Not long after, he met a businessman named Walter Sisulu. Sisulu helped Mandela learn about politics. He also helped Mandela find work with a white law firm. Mandela's salary of $4 a week was barely enough to live on. He often skipped meals and walked six miles to and from work. He finished his university study by mail.

Mandela hugs Walter Sisulu at Sisulu's 90th birthday party.

Johannesburg was a big city. Mandela saw that the nice shops and expensive cars were owned by white people. In his part of town, the houses had no electricity, running water, or telephones. The roads were dirt tracks. Gangs roamed the streets at night. Mandela began to study law so he could help people.

In this 1950 photo, poor black South Africans stand at a fence near their homes.

Joining the ANC

In 1944, Mandela married Evelyn Mase. That same year, he joined the African National Congress (ANC). The ANC was a political group. The members worked to end **DISCRIMINATION**. They wanted equal rights for all South Africans whether they were black, mixed race, Asian, or white.

In 1948, apartheid became law in South Africa. Nonwhite people had to carry a pass that told who

Vocabulary

DISCRIMINATION is the unfair practice of treating one group of people differently from other groups.

they were. They could not go to certain places. They could get only low-paying jobs. They could live only in certain areas. Most of those areas were very poor.

This is the type of pass nonwhite South Africans were forced to carry.

Whites and nonwhites were not allowed to do things together. They could not use the same bath-rooms or go to the same schools. Nonwhites could not be part of the government.

The police arrested anyone who disagreed with the government. They could harm or kill anyone they arrested. People could be held for a long time without a trial, seeing a lawyer, or a way to talk to their families.

Mandela and Oliver Tambo opened a law firm in 1952. It was the first black law firm in South Africa. They had a lot of work because they wanted to help everyone.

Protests

Mandela helped the ANC with protests. At one protest, people burned their pass books. About 8,500 people were arrested. Mandela and more than 100 other people were charged with TREASON. They could be put to death. The Treason Trial ended in 1961. Everyone was found innocent. During that time, Mandela and Evelyn's marriage ended. He married Winnie Madikizela in 1958.

At first Mandela believed in peaceful protests only. He changed his mind in 1960. During a protest that year in a town called

Vocabulary

TREASON is the crime of betraying a person's own country by going to war against it or helping enemies of the country.

Quick Fact

The Sharpeville Massacre brought international attention to the struggle against apartheid. Many countries stopped doing business with South Africa. They wanted to make the government end apartheid.

Sharpeville, the police shot and killed 69 people and wounded almost 200. Mandela felt the need to fight back. He helped organize a new wing of the ANC. It was called Umkhonto we Sizwe ("Spear of the Nation"). The members attacked government buildings. Not long after their first attack, Mandela was arrested.

This picture was taken during the Sharpeville Massacre on March 21, 1960.

CHAPTER FOUR

PRISONER NUMBER 46664

Mandela and other members of Umkhonto we Sizwe were tried in the Rivonia Trial. They were sentenced to life in prison in 1964. Others took up the fight to end apartheid. People protested all over the world. But it would be 27 years before Mandela gained his freedom.

Trial

Mandela knew that he could be sentenced to death. When he had the chance to speak, he explained why he had to use violence to try to end apartheid. At the end of his four-hour speech, he said,

"I have cherished the ideal of a democratic and free society in which all persons live together in harmony and with equal opportunities... [I]t is an ideal for which I am prepared to die."

People protest outside of the court where Mandela is sentenced to life in prison.

Life in Prison

Mandela was sent to the prison on Robben Island. It was the harshest prison in South Africa. He was given the number 466/64. This meant he was the 466th prisoner in that year, 1964. He was 46 years old. White armed guards with dogs shouted orders. He and other political prisoners had the worst food and the least freedoms. Mandela still led protests. The prisoners worked slowly. They talked and passed messages in secret.

One morning, the prisoners were given sewing needles and clothes to fix. They usually got hammers to break rocks. Soon, two people from a newspaper in London, England, arrived. They talked to Mandela and took pictures. As soon as they left, the prisoners were given hammers again. At another time, the prisoners were given better food for a few days. Then a visitor from the Red Cross arrived. The prison wanted outsiders to think that prisoners were being treated well.

Convicts work at various tasks in a prison yard.

At first Mandela could send only two letters a year and get two back. Prison

Quick Fact

The Red Cross is an agency that cares for people in battle and during natural disasters. It also helps people who are political prisoners.

guards **CENSORED** the letters. They blacked out or cut out words. Twice, Mandela got bad news. In 1968, his mother died. The following year, his oldest son, Thembi, died in a car crash. Sometimes many years passed between seeing any of his five children. He did not see his wife, Winnie, often, either. Sometimes she was in jail herself for fighting injustice.

Vocabulary

CENSORED means some information was removed because an official did not want anyone to know about it.

Freedom

In 1969, a guard told Mandela about a plan

to help him escape. Mandela did not trust the guard. He was right. It was a plan by the government to shoot and kill Mandela.

This re-creation of Mandela's prison cell is at the Nelson Mandela Museum in Qunu.

People around the world wanted Mandela freed. In 1982, he was moved to another prison. He had his own bath-room and could hug Winnie for the first time in 21 years. He began secret talks with President P. W. Botha about peace. But Botha still wanted white-only rule. In 1989, F. W. de Klerk became president. He agreed that all people should work together. Soon, political prisoners were being released. Then, in February 1990, de Klerk announced that Mandela would be released as well.

PRESIDENT MANDELA

People all over the world celebrated Mandela's freedom. Four years after his release, he was elected president of South Africa. Mandela then worked to bring the country together after so many years of hatred.

Nelson and Winnie Mandela show their happiness on the day he is finally released from prison.

Mandela and de Klerk show their Nobel medals and diplomas in December 1993.

Vocabulary

A **CONSTITUTION** is a document that describes a system of laws by which a country, state, or organization is governed.

Free at Last

Mandela walked free on Sunday, February 11, 1990. He had been in prison for 10,000 days. He was 71 years old. Mandela went right back to work. He and de Klerk worked on a new **CONSTITUTION**. It would give everyone equal rights. It was adopted in 1993. That same year, Mandela and de Klerk shared the Nobel Peace Prize.

The first free elections took place in 1994. Millions of black

Quick Fact

The Nobel Peace Prize is an annual award. Winners are selected among people all over the world whose work helps others.

South Africans voted for the first time. Mandela became president. He focused on ending poverty for black people. He also worked for peace and unity between all groups.

Mandela casts his vote in the first free South African elections.

The Truth and Reconciliation Commission

In 1995 the government set up the Truth and Reconciliation Commission (TRC). Its

RECONCILIATION.

Mandela gets the TRC's final report from Archbishop Desmond Tutu.

job was to find out about apartheid crimes. Anyone could give **EVIDENCE**. No one would be charged for crimes. Over 22,000 people spoke up. The hearings were put on radio and television in all South African languages. That gave the public the opportunity to hear what had happened in their country. After the hearings, the TRC released a report. Many people finally found out about missing or dead family and friends.

Vocabulary

EVIDENCE is spoken or visual material given to a court of law to help find the truth about something.

The TRC had an effect beyond South Africa, too. Other countries learned from the process. They established similar committees to address their own problems.

Retiring from Politics

Mandela's marriage to Winnie did not last. They divorced in 1996. When Mandela's term as president ended in 1999, he decided to retire from politics. By then he had married a third time, to Graca Machel in 1998.

In 2007, he and other retired world leaders formed a group called the Elders. They wanted to create a global village with wise and experienced leaders. They worked to address worldwide problems.

Health and Legacy

Mandela had several health problems. Some were because of a lung infection he got in prison. He was treated for cancer in 2001 and 2004. He died at his home in Qunu on December 5, 2013.

People attend a memorial for Mandela in Johannesburg on December 10, 2013.

Many people talked about what a great man Mandela was. Jacob Zuma, president of South Africa, said, "Our nation has lost its greatest son." Barack Obama, president of the United States, said, "[He] set an example that all humanity should aspire to." David Cameron, prime minister of the United Kingdom, said, "Nelson Mandela was a … hero of all time."

TIMELINE

1918: Rolihlahla Mandela is born on July 18.

1925: Mandela attends his first school. His teacher gives him the name Nelson.

About 1927: Mandela's father dies. Mandela moves to the household of Chief Jongintaba.

1941: Mandela runs away to Johannesburg to avoid an arranged marriage.

1944: Mandela joins the African National Congress (ANC) and marries Evelyn Mase.

1948: Apartheid laws are introduced in South Africa.

1956: Mandela is charged with treason. The Treason Trial begins.

1958: Mandela and Evelyn divorce. He marries Winnie Madikizela.

1960: The police kill protesters in Sharpeville. The ANC is banned from South Africa.

1961: Mandela and all others in the Treason Trial are declared innocent.

1963: Mandela and several others are tried in the Rivonia Trial.

1964: Mandela is sentenced to life imprisonment on Robben Island.

1985: Mandela begins secret talks with President P. W. Botha.

1989: Botha is replaced by F. W. de Klerk.

1990: Mandela is released from prison.

1993: Mandela and de Klerk win the Nobel Peace Prize.

1994: Mandela is elected president of South Africa.

1996: Mandela and Winnie divorce.

1998: Mandela marries Graca Machel.

1999: Mandela retires from politics.

2013: Mandela dies on December 5.

GLOSSARY

ARRESTED Held by the power of law.

ASPIRE To work toward something great.

CHIEF A person of great importance and influence in a group.

CLAN A large group of people who are related.

DEMOCRATIC Based on the idea that all people should be treated equally.

HUMANITY All people.

INFECTION A disease caused by germs that enter the body.

INNOCENT Not guilty of a crime.

MASSACRE The violent killing of many people.

PROTEST An event at which people come together to show disapproval about something.

SALARY An amount of money that an employee is paid regularly.

SENTENCED Given punishment by a court of law.

TRIBAL Of or relating to a tribe, a group of people that includes many families who have the same language, customs, and beliefs.

BOOKS

Barnham, Kay. *Nelson Mandela: Revolutionary President.* London, England: Wayland Publishers, 2014.

Kramer, Ann. *Nelson Mandela: An Extraordinary Life* (Twentieth Century History Makers). London, England: Franklin Watts, 2014.

Kramer, Barbara. *National Geographic Readers: Nelson Mandela.* Washington, DC: National Geographic Kids, 2014.

Nelson, Kadir. *Nelson Mandela.* New York, NY: HarperCollins, 2013.

Pollack, Pam, and Meg Belviso. *Who Was Nelson Mandela?* New York, NY: Penguin, 2014.

Van Wyk, Chris, ed. *Nelson Mandela: Long Walk to Freedom.* New York, NY: Roaring Brook Press, 2009.

WEBSITES

Because of the changing nature of Internet links, Rosen Publishing has developed an online list of websites related to the subject of this book. This site is updated regularly. Please use this link to access this list:

http://www.rosenlinks.com/BBB/Mand

INDEX

African National Congress (ANC), 14, 16, 17
Afrikaans, 6
apartheid, 5, 6, 14, 17, 18, 26

Botha, P. W., 22

Cameron, David, 28
coming-of-age ceremony, 11
constitution, 24

de Klerk, F. W., 22, 24

Elders, 27

human rights, 7

Machel, Graca, 27
Madikizela, Winnie, 16, 21, 22, 24, 27

Mandela, Nelson
childhood of, 8–11
as president, 4, 6, 7, 25–27
trial and imprisonment, 6, 18–22
Mase, Evelyn, 14, 16

Nobel Peace Prize, 24, 25

Obama, Barack, 28

Red Cross, 20, 21
Rivonia Trial, 18

Sharpeville Massacre, 17
Sisulu, Walter, 13
South Africa, 4, 5, 6, 8, 9, 12, 14, 16, 17, 19, 23, 25, 27, 28

Tambo, Oliver, 16
Treason Trial, 16
Truth and Reconciliation Commission (TRC), 25–26, 27

Umkhonto we Sizwe ("Spear of the Nation"), 17, 18

Xhosa language/people, 8, 9, 11

Zuma, Jacob, 28